E
P   :Peters, Sharon

    Puppet show

28

A First-Start Easy Reader

This easy reader contains only 39 different words, repeated often to help the young reader develop word recognition and interest in reading.

Basic word list for *Puppet Show*

we	show	puppet
had	made	puppets
a	arms	Jeff
the	body	Doris
cut	head	Al
out	funny	curtain
I	faces	talked
an	frog	danced
rose	mouse	sang
fell	pig	children
end	owl	laughed
over	stage	clapped
was	sign	bowed

Puppet Show

Written by Sharon Peters

Illustrated by Alana Lee

Troll Associates

ISBN 0-89375-286-X

We had a puppet show.

We made the puppets.

We cut out the puppets.

We cut out the arms.

We cut out the body.

We made the head.

We made funny faces.

The puppets made funny faces.

I made a frog.

Jeff made a mouse.

Doris made a pig.

Al made an owl.

Jeff made the stage.

Doris made the sign.

Al made the curtain.

I made funny faces.

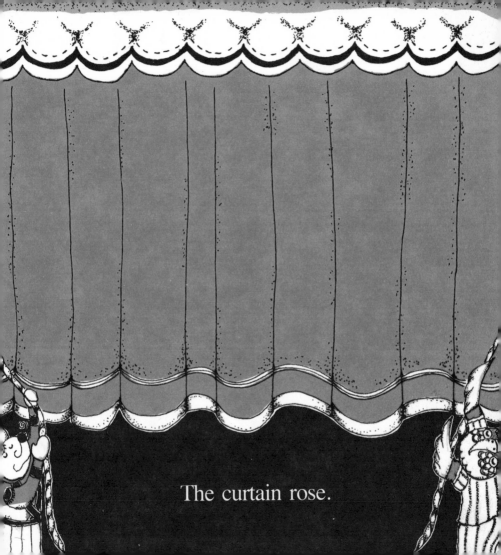

The curtain rose.

The puppets talked.

The puppets danced.

The puppets sang.

The puppets made funny faces.

The children laughed.

The children clapped.

The puppets bowed.

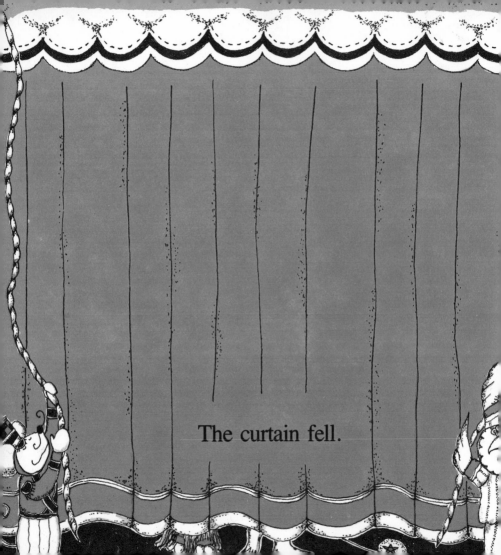

The curtain fell.

The puppet show was over.